Sit Spot and the Art of Inner Tracking

A 30-Day Challenge to Develop Your Relationship to Self, Earth, Others and the Wisdom of the Ancestors

R. Michael Trotta

Copyright © 2013 R. Michael Trotta
Sagefire Institute for Natural Coaching
Printed and Published in the United States of America
ISBN-13: 978-1493615216
ISBN-10: 1493615211

All Rights Reserved. This publication may not be reproduced, stored in a retrieval system, or transmitted in whole or in part, in any form or by any means, electronic, mechanical, photocopying, recording, or otherwise–with the exception of a reviewer who may quote brief passages in a review to be printed in a newspaper or magazine– without prior written permission from the author or publisher: michael@sagefireinstitute.com

THE WORDS BEFORE ALL ELSE: THANKSGIVING

The People
Love and gratitude to my wife Lynn and to all my family. Gratitude to my teachers and mentors, especially Mark Morey, Jon Young, Uncle Paul, and Martha Beck for showing me how to see into the dark. To my Sacred Fire brothers and to my nephews Sam, Charlie, and Rocco. Thank you to my big sister Betsy Rapoport for making this and so many other projects of mine make sense to the rest of the world. Thank you Kelly Eide, Margaret Webb, and June Bayha for helping me to breathe new life into these pages.

The Earth
Thanks to my Sit Spots, all of them, to the trees and plants (big and small), to the four-leggeds, winged-ones and even the creepy crawlers (big and small), and to all the living and not so living things that make up the earth, thank you for making every single sit worth going to.

The Fire
Undoubtedly one of my greatest teachers, it is because of you that "the fire burns brightly now," and for that I am most grateful. I shall do my best to humbly serve others as you have served me, for "I am of the people."

The Waters
Thank you, waters, for bringing balance to my life, to my fire, and for teaching me patience and surrender.

The Great Mystery
To the seen and unseen Mysteries that are woven into all things and reflect back to each one of us exactly what we need to know if only we take the time to pay attention–thank you.

The Future Generations
To my dear, sweet Oonagh Rose, thank you for giving me more reason than ever before to do this work in service of you and the generations still to come. You are the light upon the horizon.

CONTENTS

- HOW TO USE THIS JOURNAL 10
- HOW TO CHOOSE A SIT SPOT 12
- SOME COMMON QUESTIONS ABOUT SIT SPOT 14
- FILLING OUT YOUR SIT SPOT JOURNAL 16
- DAY 1 - SIT SPOT JOURNAL 26
  - CORE ROUTINES OF NATURE AWARENESS–DAILY PRACTICE: *GRATITUDE* 28
- DAY 2 - SIT SPOT JOURNAL 30
  - CORE ROUTINES OF NATURE AWARENESS–DAILY PRACTICE: *OWL EYES* 32
- DAY 3 - SIT SPOT JOURNAL 34
  - CORE ROUTINES OF NATURE AWARENESS–DAILY PRACTICE: *LANDMARKS AND HAZARDS* 36
- DAY 4 - SIT SPOT JOURNAL 38
  - CORE ROUTINES OF NATURE AWARENESS–DAILY PRACTICE: *CHILDHOOD PASSIONS* 40
- DAY 5 - SIT SPOT JOURNAL 42
  - CORE ROUTINES OF NATURE AWARENESS–DAILY PRACTICE: *LEAF LINE-UP* 44
- DAY 6 - SIT SPOT JOURNAL 46
  - CORE ROUTINES OF NATURE AWARENESS–DAILY PRACTICE: *KNOW YOUR NEIGHBORS* 48
- DAY 7 - SIT SPOT JOURNAL 50
  - CORE ROUTINES OF NATURE AWARENESS–DAILY PRACTICE: *GET CREATIVE!* 52
- DAY 8 - SIT SPOT JOURNAL 54
  - CORE ROUTINES OF NATURE AWARENESS–DAILY PRACTICE: *GRATITUDE* 58
- DAY 9 - SIT SPOT JOURNAL 60
  - CORE ROUTINES OF NATURE AWARENESS–DAILY PRACTICE: *DEER EARS* 64
- DAY 10 - SIT SPOT JOURNAL 66

CORE ROUTINES OF NATURE AWARENESS–DAILY PRACTICE:
MAPPING TREES & PLANTS 68

DAY 11 - SIT SPOT JOURNAL 70

CORE ROUTINES OF NATURE AWARENESS–DAILY PRACTICE:
THE ART OF QUESTIONING 74

DAY 12 - SIT SPOT JOURNAL 76

CORE ROUTINES OF NATURE AWARENESS–DAILY PRACTICE:
THREE PERSPECTIVES 80

DAY 13 - SIT SPOT JOURNAL 82

CORE ROUTINES OF NATURE AWARENESS–DAILY PRACTICE:
KNOW YOUR NEIGHBORS 86

DAY 14 - SIT SPOT JOURNAL 88

CORE ROUTINES OF NATURE AWARENESS–DAILY PRACTICE:
GET CREATIVE! 92

DAY 15 - SIT SPOT JOURNAL 94

CORE ROUTINES OF NATURE AWARENESS–DAILY PRACTICE:
SHADOWTUDE GRATITUDE 98

DAY 16 - SIT SPOT JOURNAL 100

CORE ROUTINES OF NATURE AWARENESS–DAILY PRACTICE:
THE SENSE MEDITATION 104

DAY 17 - SIT SPOT JOURNAL 106

CORE ROUTINES OF NATURE AWARENESS–DAILY PRACTICE:
MAPPING BIRDS AND MAMMALS 110

DAY 18 - SIT SPOT JOURNAL 112

CORE ROUTINES OF NATURE AWARENESS–DAILY PRACTICE:
AWARENESS CHALLENGE 116

DAY 19 - SIT SPOT JOURNAL 118

CORE ROUTINES OF NATURE AWARENESS–DAILY PRACTICE:
SPIRIT DRAWINGS 122

DAY 20 - SIT SPOT JOURNAL 124

CORE ROUTINES OF NATURE AWARENESS–DAILY PRACTICE:
KNOW YOUR NEIGHBORS 128

DAY 21 - SIT SPOT JOURNAL 130

CORE ROUTINES OF NATURE AWARENESS–DAILY PRACTICE: *GET CREATIVE!* 134

DAY 22 - SIT SPOT JOURNAL 136

CORE ROUTINES OF NATURE AWARENESS–DAILY PRACTICE: *GRATITUDE* 140

DAY 23 - SIT SPOT JOURNAL 142

CORE ROUTINES OF NATURE AWARENESS–DAILY PRACTICE: *FOX WALKING* 146

DAY 24 - SIT SPOT JOURNAL 148

CORE ROUTINES OF NATURE AWARENESS–DAILY PRACTICE: *MAPPING* 152

DAY 25 - SIT SPOT JOURNAL 154

CORE ROUTINES OF NATURE AWARENESS–DAILY PRACTICE: *AWARENESS CHALLENGE* 158

DAY 26 - SIT SPOT JOURNAL 160

CORE ROUTINES OF NATURE AWARENESS–DAILY PRACTICE: *DRAW WHAT YOU FEEL* 164

DAY 27 - SIT SPOT JOURNAL 166

CORE ROUTINES OF NATURE AWARENESS–DAILY PRACTICE: *KNOW YOUR NEIGHBORS* 170

DAY 28 - SIT SPOT JOURNAL 172

CORE ROUTINES OF NATURE AWARENESS–DAILY PRACTICE: *GET CREATIVE!* 176

DAY 29 - SIT SPOT JOURNAL 178

CORE ROUTINES OF NATURE AWARENESS–DAILY PRACTICE: *HONORING AND COMMITMENTS* 182

DAY 30 - SIT SPOT JOURNAL 184

CORE ROUTINES OF NATURE AWARENESS–DAILY PRACTICE: *GRATITUDE* 188

ABOUT THE AUTHOR 192

INTRODUCTION

Welcome to Sit Spot and the Art of Inner Tracking. This 30-Day Challenge is more than just a journal. It's more than a coaching program. It's a path, a journey. In many ways, it's a hero's journey, one that will lead you from the known into the unknown and back with unforeseen treasures. It will guide you into two distinct yet deeply related practices that will merge and serve as a powerful ally to help you fulfill your intention for this and many other journeys life has to offer you.

Sit Spot is the simple act of finding a particular place outdoors where you sit quietly and observe. By taking yourself out of your regular daily routine and reconnecting with the rhythms of the natural world, you begin to recalibrate and reconnect with your own true nature. By spending time outside in this way, and by consciously practicing your ability to observe, you will strengthen your awareness. Think of awareness as a muscle.

Often, we're not fully aware of what's going on inside us and around us; we've let that muscle atrophy. The Sit Spot Challenge will be your personal trainer for the next 30 days, helping you rebuild and retrain this crucial ability.

Like Sit Spot, Inner Tracking comes from humble beginnings. Our native ancestors relied upon their ability to follow and read the messages written upon the earth. What animal made those footprints? What does a change in wind direction mean? How can an animal's movement guide me to water? What can the language of birds tell me about my own survival? Tracking all these things allowed our earlier hunter-gatherer relatives to live and thrive. These survival strategies dominated our way of being. That's to say, we became a species that thrived by observing and questioning.

However, we have largely disconnected from a conscious relationship with the earth. Since we no longer need our ancestral tracking abilities for our daily survival, we use them less and less, and often fail to see how all things are interrelated. That's why Inner Tracking is so important; in combination with Sit Spot, we can learn to turn our natural ability to observe and question toward our inner landscape. Here we may track our deeper truth in and out of the shadows, build relationship to our emotions and thoughts, and discover the treasures that allow us to create a life and world that serves ourselves, others, and future generations.

While you can take the 30-Day Sit Spot Challenge alone, it was designed to be shared. Another thing we've lost as a result of our disconnect from nature is an understanding of the vital importance of community. I hope you'll seek out some fellow adventurers and truth seekers with whom you can share your stories as you go.

On a final note–and I make no bones about it–you get out of this program what you put into it. And why limit your Sit Spot to 30 days? Many have returned to this challenge several times and some...well, they're still out there.

Happy sitting!

HOW TO USE THIS JOURNAL

The practice of Sit Spot has been found all over the world and I'd be lying if I said it's always done the same way. Every culture, every tribe, and I'll go so far as to say every individual has their own unique way of making the basics of the practice work for them. I invite you to do the same...in just 30 short days from now. For now, however, please follow the practices as outlined in the journal. As time goes on, you'll discover new tools and routines that will help you develop your unique Sit Spot savvy.

Before actually beginning the 30-Day Challenge, please be sure to carefully read pages 10 to 23.

Then, every day, for the next 30 days (and I do suggest you commit to 30 days in a row), fill out the relevant journal pages **after** you have gone to your Sit Spot. The first two pages for each day will be the same throughout the journal. The questions you'll find there are the same ones native trackers have been asking for millennia. You can use them to track what's going on around you as well as inside you. I'll explain more about these questions in the coming pages. For now, all you need to know is that the goal of these questions is to re-pattern your brain by training you to look at the world in a different way: Nature's way.

After the first week, you will find two additional blank pages for each day. Use these to do some reflective journaling in whatever way feels best. Draw pictures, record your thoughts, observations, questions, and whatever else came to you during your Sit Spot (see journal example on pages 18 to 21). It's important, however, that you continue to fill out the first two pages for each day until you've finished the 30 days.

In addition to your journaling pages, you'll find two more pages for each day that offer practices and challenges to deepen your relationship with your Sit Spot and the natural world. These are the core routines of nature awareness.

Before heading out to your Sit Spot, be sure to review the journal pages for the day. Leave the journal behind when you go out to sit. After you have competed your Sit Spot, return and fill out the day's journal entry. I find it helpful to fill out the journal immediately after my sit is over while any takeaways are fresh in my mind.

That's it. That's a lot. The more closely you follow this rhythm, the more you'll get from the experience. After 30 days, you may feel called to experiment with the practice of Sit Spot and find ways that work for you as an individual.

I've done my best to keep this journal simple. I invite you to make it your own right from the start. If writing full paragraphs suits you, please do so. If you prefer to write in bullet points or poetry, do that! It's your call. And please, feel free to bring color to the otherwise white pages of this journal by cutting and pasting photos into it or making colorful sketches of things you find and are curious about while at your Sit Spot: feathers, leaves, flowers, hair, photos of tracks, etc. My own journals are filled with such things and I find them to be of great value today, years later, both as a resource of valuable information as well as a memento of experiences from my Sit Spot journey.

Think of your journal as a kind of elder or teacher. Not just any teacher, mind you, but one who understands the concepts of mentoring in the native sense of the word. Native teaching, coaching, or mentoring is reflective of the natural world: free from judgment and focused on drawing the answers from your own wisdom, not the elder's. If for some reason you can't go to your Sit Spot, write in your journal anyway. Fill out whatever parts you can, reflecting on how you feel about not going to your Sit Spot, why you didn't go, and whether or not you see a pattern in your thinking and behavior. Do these patterns and behaviors show up elsewhere in your life? Remember, this journaling process is about awareness, not judgment.

HOW TO CHOOSE A SIT SPOT

First and foremost, find a place that you can easily, safely, and conveniently visit every day. It's better to have your Sit Spot in a "less desirable" location close to home (less than 20 paces from your back porch) than it is to have one in the "perfect" location a mile down the road. Convenience and safety are the top priorities.

When at all possible, try to find a place that animals are attracted to, in other words, one that provides wildlife with water, shelter, and food. Transition areas, where fields meet tree lines, are often hotspots for a variety of species and afford you an excellent view. If your backyard has none of these to offer, make them! A bird feeder is a simple way to attract wildlife to your Sit Spot!

When actually going to your Sit Spot, move as quietly as possible; the more noise you make, the more you'll disturb creatures nearby. Fox Walking, Owl Eyes, and other routines of awareness explained later in this manual will help you with this. But reading about them and actually practicing them are altogether different. Why do I say this? Because nine times out of ten, when people tell me that things aren't going the way they hoped or that they're not seeing anything at their Sit Spot, they tell me, "No, I'm not actually doing the core routines. I did read about them, though!" Reading alone won't cut it!

The number one reason people stop going to their Sit Spot before they've built a meaningful relationship to it is because they're not comfortable–and the main reason they're uncomfortable is because they're not dressed appropriately for the weather. If you find yourself physically uncomfortable while at your Sit Spot, reevaluate what you're wearing. You may need an extra layer of clothing, rain gear, a hat to keep off glare, or even a blanket.

Sit Spot is a place for you to be with nature. Leave distractions at home, especially this journal. However, if bringing a cup of tea or coffee will make your experience more pleasurable, well, by all means do so.

The rest of this journal is designed to guide you into a powerful relationship with the practice of Sit Spot. While there are no rules around how to do your Sit Spot, these basic guidelines will help you get the most out of it. By the end of the 30-Day Challenge, if you have followed and practiced these suggestions, you'll have built a solid foundation that will change the way you look at both your outer and inner worlds.

SOME COMMON QUESTIONS ABOUT SIT SPOT

What if I live in the city?
Great! There is plenty of nature to observe even in the busiest city. If you're finding it super-difficult to find a quiet Sit Spot, however, you may wish to have two Sit Spots; one nearby that you can visit during the week and the other perhaps a little farther away where there's more of a habitat for wild animals. Visit this one for longer periods of time when possible.

How often do I go and when?
Visit your Sit Spot every day if you can and vary the times of day that you go. Sunrise sits, sunset sits, midnight and mid-day sits–mix it up. See how the rhythms of nature vary with the time of day and the time of year. Does weather affect anything? How about the phase of the moon? In time, you may be amazed at how much is influenced by nature and its cycles.

Do I have to sit on the ground? Can I sit on a chair?
Sit in whatever way is most comfortable for you. Some people prefer sitting directly on the earth for the connection they feel. Others choose to sit in a chair. Like nature, there is no right or wrong way.

What if it's raining?
What a great opportunity to be a part of such an incredible event! It's up to you to decide if you're going to join the party or not. But here's where some inner tracking will come in. So, it's raining out (or snowing, hailing, freezing, boiling, or whatever the inclement weather). What are you making that mean? Where else in your life are you not getting into life because of the thought of getting wet or being a little uncomfortable is too much for you?

Can I do my Sit Spot inside?
You can, but it sort of defeats the purpose, so no, not really.

How long do I sit for?
Twenty minutes is good for starters. A simple rule of thumb regarding the effectiveness of Sit Spot is: the longer you stay and the more often you go, the more effective it will be. On average, it takes about 20 minutes for the animals to return to their baseline behaviors after a human has passed by. One of the goals of Sit Spot is to be in nature long enough to observe baseline; this is when you begin to gain access to the deeper layers of both self and the natural world. However, most people find it difficult to sit for this long when they first begin to practice Sit Spot. Be patient with yourself. In time, sitting longer becomes an easy and welcomed practice and you'll find that sitting long enough to see baseline return to the environment is no problem at all.

Can I change my Sit Spot from day to day?
The power of Sit Spot comes from getting to know one place really well. Therefore, I recommend that you use the same spot every day.

This may sound like a stupid question, but what do I do during Sit Spot? Do I just sit? Take notes in my journal? What?
Not a stupid question at all. Start by finding your Sit Spot as outlined on page 12 (How to Choose a Sit Spot). Go to it and sit. Do what feels right–breathe, look around, close your eyes and listen, meditate. As you get further into the journal, you'll be taught new skills to practice while at your Sit Spot. For now, just enjoy being there and being as present as possible. You can fill out your journal when you're done.

FILLING OUT YOUR SIT SPOT JOURNAL

Data:
This one is pretty straightforward. You can find moon phases and sunrise and sunset times online or in local newspapers. If you wake up with the sun, simply take note of the time. Becoming aware of these patterns will quickly help you to sync yourself to the rhythms by which all other living creatures besides humans live. Isn't that astonishing? All other living creatures on the planet live and die by a completely different flow from most of us humans. I think I just blew my own mind.

My Intention / Motivation:
If you want to master Inner Tracking, you've got to know what you're tracking. That is, you must be clear on what it is you hope to create: quietness of mind, a deeper connection to nature, a better understanding of why you and your spouse keep arguing and what to do about it? First figure out what you're looking to track, then set that **intention** before going to your Sit Spot. Carry that intention with you as you travel to your Sit Spot and then let it go, trusting that what needs to show up, will. Understanding your **motivation** is also important. I like to think of motivation as the intention *behind* the intention, i.e., the feeling that is driving the intention. Is that feeling pushing you toward a deeper relationship with something, or is it causing you to avoid a deeper relationship? See the Sit Spot Journal Sample Pages for an example.

What I noticed in nature:
Use all your senses to convey what you observed while at your Sit Spot. Describe more than what you saw; write down the smells, sounds, physical sensations and even tastes you experienced while there. Take note of anything that captured your attention: animals, winds, rain, temperatures, tracks, etc. Feel free to share anything you noticed about interactions you observed or patterns you become aware of.

What I noticed within myself:
Just as you've made observations of the outer landscape, now do the same of your inner landscape. Take note of any strong feel-

ings, sensations, thoughts, judgments, and challenges that present themselves to you on a physical, intellectual, or emotional level. There is no one right way to do this–or any of the rest of the journal, for that matter. Experiment and seek what works best for you.

What this is teaching me / telling me:
What did you learn from your observations? What does it tell you when a bird that was singing away one minute, suddenly goes quiet seconds before a hawk flies by? What does it tell you when you observe ten times more animal activity during the second half of your Sit Spot than you did during the first half?

Where I see this reflected in my life:
When you set an intention for a deeper knowing and turn to nature for answers, you get the wisdom reflected to you in a pure and nonjudgmental way. Because you're the one making meaning from what shows up at your Sit Spot, you can trust that the answers you get are yours and not another person's judgments, projections, or values.

Questions and things to pay attention to:
What questions do you have as a result of your visit to your Sit Spot? They may be about something you saw: a bird, tree, or plant. They may be about what was going on for you internally, such as, "Every time I try to get quiet, why do my concerns about money start showing up?" You may also want to jot down a few things to pay attention to at your next visit. For example: "At my next Sit Spot I want to see if that track I saw had four toes or five and if there were nails at the end of each toe." Or, it may be something from your inner landscape that you will want to pay more attention to, such as, "I've noticed that when I give thanks at my Sit Spot, I find it easier to sit quietly. I want to test this and see what happens."

Additional reflection pages:
After the first week, you'll find two additional journal pages for each day. You may use these pages in whatever way you see fit. Many people use this space to write down stream-of-consciousness reflections.

SAMPLE - SIT SPOT JOURNAL

DATE: July 31st　　　TIME: 6:45 am – 7:30ish

SUNRISE: 5:29 am　　SUNSET: 8:31 pm

MOON PHASE: waxing gibbous

WEATHER: Clear skies, 75 degrees when I checked at 8am, there's been no rain for over a week, rain predicted for tomorrow

My Intention / Motivation:

My intention was to gain clarity around how to better relate to my son who seems to want nothing to do with me lately. My motivation is to get closer to him. I love him but so often it seems I drive him away. So, my motivation is love—that's where I am coming from. But thinking on it, I can also recognize some fear too—fear that I may lose him.

What I noticed in nature:

The river seemed extra loud today, bubbling and gurgling as it flowed in spite of it being lower than usual. I saw a fawn walking on the far side of it—flicking its tail and eating greens. There was a lot of bird song but I'm not sure which kind of birds—a high pitched chipping sound is how I'd describe it. The sun was brilliant as it beamed through the tree tops revealing a misty glow above the water. The earth itself felt dry and parched. I found a feather—fuzzy—I think it's from an owl.

What I noticed within myself:

-I noticed that I was feeling sad watching the fawn.
-I couldn't help thinking it was all alone in the world.
-My attention kept getting pulled to the sound of the river, I could literally hear the rocks at the bottom making noise.
-The first 15 min. I felt really distracted, couldn't stop thinking about all the work I have to do today.

What this is telling me / teaching me:

Thinking about the fawn eating those greens all by itself—it's obvious I know but what it has me thinking is that though it's young, it's at the point where it's ready to eat by itself—no longer suckling.

The river—there's something in its noise, its music, that required the lack of rain to reveal it—kind of like it needs less in order to become more...

Where I see this reflected in my life:

The fawn is totally like my son, more independent than I give him credit for and the river, well maybe I need to be like the water—less so that my son can be more.

Questions and things to pay attention to:

-What is my sadness trying to say to me?
-Owl feather?

SAMPLE - REFLECTION PAGES

July 31st

You know, I just reread what I wrote on the previous page and I can't stop thinking about the fawn and the bird song. It was "song" not alarms that the birds were making. They were at peace or at least I should say there was nothing going on that was of danger to them. And if that's true, it's likely there was nothing of danger for the fawn either.

The fawn was in fact, flicking its tail, grazing lazily on this and that. It actually seemed quite content. It was me who brought sadness and even fear into those woods.

Sadness and fear—mine, not the deer's. Not my son's. Mine. What am I afraid of? Sad of?

Fear—I'm afraid something will happen to my son, that he'll get hurt or that I won't be able to stop him from getting hurt. Reality is, he will likely get hurt—that's a part of a life well lived, isn't it?

Sadness—maybe it's more that he wants to be independent of me—yes it's a good thing of course but... Wow! The thought of him not needing me... Oh, man! The dry earth! That's it. I'm afraid and sad about what it will mean to me when he doesn't need me anymore—dried up and useless.

REFLECTION PAGES

Dried up and useless dad—really though, I'm acting like that now—no wonder he wants more space from me. I would too!

My next intention is going to be around gaining a better understanding of what I want my life to be like rather that what I don't want it to be like and perhaps ask myself what I need to focus my energy on more rather than focusing it all on my son who is becoming more independent (which is what I really want for him anyway).

Mr. Owl, where are you?

DAILY PRACTICES

In addition to your daily Sit Spot journal pages, you will find a "Daily Practice." These core routines of nature awareness will help you to build your inner and outer relationship to both the natural world and thus, to yourself. You can apply these time-tested practices to just about any area of your life. Practicing gratitude, developing sensory awareness, conscious movement, and cultivating creativity are all pathways to discovery and expressing your true nature.

Some of these practices may push your edges. Good! They're meant to take you outside of your comfort zone and reveal to you your blind spots. If you're looking for a program that will reinforce your old ways of being, this ain't it! If that's what you want, ask for your money back now. But if you're willing to explore the edges so that you can expand them, you should do just fine.

As with everything in this 30-Day challenge, pay attention to how these daily practices make you feel. Which practices speak to you and which don't? Be sure to document these observations; they are all tracks in the sand, each one leading you closer to your true self.

It is my hope that at the end of the 30-Day Sit Spot Challenge, you will have discovered a treasure trove of tools and daily practices that you can utilize independently, anytime, anywhere. Used consistently, these tools will constantly realign you with your true nature and your authentic self.

DAY 1 - SIT SPOT JOURNAL

DATE: TIME:

SUNRISE: SUNSET:

MOON PHASE:

WEATHER:

My Intention / Motivation:

What I noticed in nature:

What I noticed within myself:

What this is telling me / teaching me:

Where I see this reflected in my life:

Questions and things to pay attention to:

CORE ROUTINES OF NATURE AWARENESS

DAILY PRACTICE: GRATITUDE

Take some time to think of the small moments that you experience in nature that make life special. The smell of a pine forest or a freshly mowed lawn perhaps? Walking barefoot on a sandy shore or the sweet taste of wild raspberries? Allow your senses to guide you as you complete the sentence starter, "I love it when..." as many times as you can. "I love it when a butterfly uncurls its long tongue (proboscis) to drink the nectar from a flower." "I love it when everything feels quieter right before it snows." Go wild and really open up with your truth: "I love it when I drive down the highway and the smell of skunk fills the car."

"What is life?
It is the flash of a firefly in the night.
It is the breath of the buffalo in the wintertime.
It is the little shadow which runs across the grass and
loses itself in the sunset."

- Crowfoot,
Blackfoot Warrior and Orator 1830 - 1890

DAY 2 - SIT SPOT JOURNAL

DATE: TIME:

SUNRISE: SUNSET:

MOON PHASE:

WEATHER:

My Intention / Motivation:

What I noticed in nature:

What I noticed within myself:

What this is telling me / teaching me:

Where I see this reflected in my life:

Questions and things to pay attention to:

CORE ROUTINES OF NATURE AWARENESS

DAILY PRACTICE: OWL EYES

For most of us, seeing the world through a highly focused, limited field of view is the result of the conditioning we received in grade school. Though such focused attention and vision may have allowed us to learn to read and write, when it becomes our dominant way of seeing, we limit our awareness of everything else. In fact, you are narrowing your ability to take in a bigger picture right now simply by reading these words. In order to develop a greater awareness of nature, or anything else for that matter, it is absolutely necessary to be able to use both focused and wide-angle vision and learn to switch consciously between the two. To better understand this, try the following practice:

FIRST: Focus your vision on a fixed point in front of you.

SECOND: Soften your focused gaze and begin to take in as much as you can to the right and left of that point without moving your head or eyes. Allow your vision to begin to soften.

THIRD: With your eyes still trained on the original point (but not focused on it), also take in as much as you can above and below that point.

Your field of view, though slightly less focused, should now be taking in quite a bit more than it was while focused on the fixed point. This is what is called "Owl Eyes" or "wide-angle vision."

Challenge:

For the next week, practice using Owl Eyes while at your Sit Spot. Experiment going in and out of it. Try using it in other places as well: at the gym, walking through the mall, while reading a book. See where it works and where it doesn't. Pay attention to what it allows you to do while in nature and ask yourself the following questions:

How might using wide-angle vision be linked to wilderness survival (for both animals and humans)?

How could using wide-angle vision serve me in my daily living (when not at Sit Spot)?

Do I notice any shifts in my emotions or mood when I'm in Owl Eyes versus focused vision? Explain.

Metaphorically speaking, how might I use Owl Eyes as an approach to problem solving?

DAY 3 - SIT SPOT JOURNAL

DATE: TIME:

SUNRISE: SUNSET:

MOON PHASE:

WEATHER:

My Intention / Motivation:

What I noticed in nature:

What I noticed within myself:

What this is telling me / teaching me:

Where I see this reflected in my life:

Questions and things to pay attention to:

CORE ROUTINES OF NATURE AWARENESS

DAILY PRACTICE: LANDMARKS AND HAZARDS

Mapping your Sit Spot area will offer you countless benefits and endless opportunities to improve your knowledge of place and powers of observation, and it can be lots of fun too! For your first mapping exercise, begin by picturing yourself looking down on your Sit Spot. Mark that spot in the center of the page.

Next, add in any significant landmarks (what this means is up to you) and potential hazards (for example, the wasp nest in the tree, the pile of lumber with rusty nails in the corner of the yard, the neighbor's rocket launcher shooting range). For orientation purposes, be certain to add in a compass rose, indicating the four directions. Try doing this all from memory. Resist the urge to run outside and double check yourself. Tomorrow, when you visit your Sit Spot, you will notice the blind spots that were out of your awareness. Feel free to return to the map and make any corrections.

"We were taught to sit still and enjoy the silence.
We were taught to use our organs of smell,
to look when apparently there was nothing to see and to
listen intently when all was seemingly quiet."

- Luther Standing Bear

DAY 4 - SIT SPOT JOURNAL

DATE: TIME:

SUNRISE: SUNSET:

MOON PHASE:

WEATHER:

My Intention / Motivation:

What I noticed in nature:

What I noticed within myself:

What this is telling me / teaching me:

Where I see this reflected in my life:

Questions and things to pay attention to:

CORE ROUTINES OF NATURE AWARENESS

DAILY PRACTICE: CHILDHOOD PASSIONS

Take a moment to create a list of the games and activities you played as a child. But wait, I don't mean Monopoly or Pac-Man. I'm talking about the games that no one really ever taught you how to play. The games that you figured out on your own and for which you made up the "rules" as you went along. The games that you might have played all day long, if you hadn't been called inside. For example: building forts (with sticks or blankets), hide-and-seek, making mud pies, tree climbing, and so forth.

Use the space provided to create as complete a list as possible. Recruit a friend to help you if you like. When you're finished, for each activity listed, identify an aspect of human survival you were learning / enacting as a result of engaging in these activities. For example: building forts taught you about shelter and protection from the elements. Hide-and-seek is similar to hunting and gathering, requiring awareness. Making mud pies is like cooking food. Simply splashing in puddles even helped teach you an understanding of your impact on the world around you and how the earth responds to you. Think back on how you felt playing these games compared to ones with rigid rules or ones that required adult referees.

Feel free to add to this list any time you remember something. Ask others to share with you the things they did as children for hours on end, without formal instruction or adult guidance.

Watch them carefully as they speak. Track their body language and ask yourself: What does this mean?

"What did you do as a child that made the hours pass like minutes? Herein lies the key to your earthly pursuits."

- C.G. Jung

DAY 5 - SIT SPOT JOURNAL

DATE: TIME:

SUNRISE: SUNSET:

MOON PHASE:

WEATHER:

My Intention / Motivation:

What I noticed in nature:

What I noticed within myself:

What this is telling me / teaching me:

Where I see this reflected in my life:

Questions and things to pay attention to:

CORE ROUTINES OF NATURE AWARENESS

DAILY PRACTICE: LEAF LINE-UP

First, collect five leaves from the same tree. Choose one of them to be your suspect, I mean, subject. Carefully study the leaf for one minute, then put it away and give yourself five minutes to draw it. When time is up, take all the leaves out and line them up next to one another. Could your drawing be used to identify the leaf you drew if it were in a line-up? Test it out. Show someone your drawing and see if he or she can select the suspect among the pile. If yes, great! Ask your friend what clues in your drawing helped identify it. If not, ask yourself: What would it take to identify the one leaf among the many?

Keep collecting interesting natural objects that you find at your Sit Spot and elsewhere. Create a special space for them, your own nature museum. Your nature museum will serve an important role in your development of a deeper awareness.

DAY 6 - SIT SPOT JOURNAL

DATE: TIME:

SUNRISE: SUNSET:

MOON PHASE:

WEATHER:

My Intention / Motivation:

What I noticed in nature:

What I noticed within myself:

What this is telling me / teaching me:

Where I see this reflected in my life:

Questions and things to pay attention to:

CORE ROUTINES OF NATURE AWARENESS

DAILY PRACTICE: KNOW YOUR NEIGHBORS

Field guides are an invaluable tool in the process of developing a relationship with nature. Think of them as the elders of the village, the wisdom keepers. Today, visit with them in order to fill in the information below. Feel free to use the internet if you don't have a field guide on hand, but as with any fact-finding mission, consider the source. Try spending no more than 15 minutes reading and researching and no more than 15 minutes journaling the information.

Select a bird species local to your area for this exercise.

COMMON NAME   **SCIENTIFIC NAME**

Draw and label identifying characteristics (field marks):

Fill in the spaces below from your memory only, if you can.

Physical Description:

Habitat:

Behavior:

Diet:

Range:

Relationship to Native People:

Other Curious Facts:

DAY 7 - SIT SPOT JOURNAL

DATE: TIME:

SUNRISE: SUNSET:

MOON PHASE:

WEATHER:

My Intention / Motivation:

What I noticed in nature:

What I noticed within myself:

What this is telling me / teaching me:

Where I see this reflected in my life:

Questions and things to pay attention to:

CORE ROUTINES OF NATURE AWARENESS

DAILY PRACTICE: GET CREATIVE!

Use the space provided in any way that will help you deepen your relationship to your Sit Spot, nature, and yourself. Jot down poems, songs, maps, words of thanksgiving, notes, questions, a Sit Spot story–whatever you feel inspired to do!

DAY 8 - SIT SPOT JOURNAL

DATE: TIME:

SUNRISE: SUNSET:

MOON PHASE:

WEATHER:

My Intention / Motivation:

What I noticed in nature:

What I noticed within myself:

What this is telling me / teaching me:

Where I see this reflected in my life:

Questions and things to pay attention to:

SIT SPOT JOURNAL

REFLECTION PAGES

CORE ROUTINES OF NATURE AWARENESS

DAILY PRACTICE: GRATITUDE

Think of something in nature for which you are truly grateful. It may be a special place, a particular tree, an animal that you feel connected to, the sky, the rain, the moon, anything that is of importance to you. Now, write it a thank-you note. Let it know what it means to you. Let it know how the world is a better place for its being a part of creation.

DAY 9 - SIT SPOT JOURNAL

DATE: TIME:

SUNRISE: SUNSET:

MOON PHASE:

WEATHER:

My Intention / Motivation:

What I noticed in nature:

What I noticed within myself:

What this is telling me / teaching me:

Where I see this reflected in my life:

Questions and things to pay attention to:

SIT SPOT JOURNAL

REFLECTION PAGES

CORE ROUTINES OF NATURE AWARENESS

DAILY PRACTICE: DEER EARS

Deer, like many other prey animals, have the ability to turn their ears in such a way that they can locate sounds in a 360° field. As humans and predators, our ears are arranged to take in sound from a much narrower field of view (or sound). By slowing down and consciously tuning into our hearing, we can easily expand the level of our awareness. To better understand this, try the following practice:

FIRST: The next time you've settled in at your Sit Spot, close your eyes and take a few deep and relaxing breaths.

SECOND: With your eyes still closed, take in one sound that grabs your attention.

THIRD: While maintaining an awareness of the first sound, begin to add additional sounds to your awareness so that you can

hear as many noises as you can at one time. Notice how you experience these sounds in your mind's eye.

FOURTH: Open your eyes and go into a soft gaze. Practice using both Owl Eyes and Deer Ears simultaneously.

Challenge:
Practice this at your Sit Spot for the next week. Experiment using both Owl Eyes and Deer Ears away from Sit Spot too. Try practicing while walking. Notice how it affects the way you walk and consider the following questions:

In what ways might using Deer Ears help me become better connected with nature?

Consider the difference between how a predatory animal uses its sense of hearing versus a prey animal (mountain lion versus deer, for example). What might the costs and benefits to each be? How might the way an animal uses its sense of hearing influence its behaviors and survival strategies?

Metaphorically speaking, where in my life might I benefit from widening my ability to hear?

DAY 10 - SIT SPOT JOURNAL

DATE: TIME:

SUNRISE: SUNSET:

MOON PHASE:

WEATHER:

My Intention / Motivation:

What I noticed in nature:

What I noticed within myself:

What this is telling me / teaching me:

Where I see this reflected in my life:

Questions and things to pay attention to:

CORE ROUTINES OF NATURE AWARENESS

DAILY PRACTICE: MAPPING TREES & PLANTS

The title pretty much says it all. Redraw your original map, complete with significant landmarks and any changes that you have recognized since last week. Next, in addition to the landmarks, identify the trees and plants. How you do this is up to you. Names aren't important but feel free to use them if it helps you (you can call it a red oak, you can call it Quercus rubra or you can call it "George"; it's up to you).

Descriptions work too! Sometimes they're even better. Notice the different species of plants and trees that are growing around your Sit Spot. Again, the real fun will come tomorrow, when you can see how much more there is than you had ever realized.

DAY 11 - SIT SPOT JOURNAL

DATE: TIME:

SUNRISE: SUNSET:

MOON PHASE:

WEATHER:

My Intention / Motivation:

What I noticed in nature:

What I noticed within myself:

What this is telling me / teaching me:

Where I see this reflected in my life:

Questions and things to pay attention to:

SIT SPOT JOURNAL

REFLECTION PAGES

CORE ROUTINES OF NATURE AWARENESS

DAILY PRACTICE: THE ART OF QUESTIONING

Select a natural object from your nature museum or go outside and find something interesting. Go on! I'll wait....Your challenge is to ask 100 questions about the object. Yes, yes, I know what you're thinking, "Only a hundred?" Yes, only a hundred. I thought I'd go easy on you this time. Feel free to have someone help you and pay attention to the ways in which you limit your ability to ask questions. Notice what works for you to help yourself move past those limitations. Good luck!

DAY 12 - SIT SPOT JOURNAL

DATE: TIME:

SUNRISE: SUNSET:

MOON PHASE:

WEATHER:

My Intention / Motivation:

What I noticed in nature:

What I noticed within myself:

What this is telling me / teaching me:

Where I see this reflected in my life:

Questions and things to pay attention to:

SIT SPOT JOURNAL

REFLECTION PAGES

CORE ROUTINES OF NATURE AWARENESS

DAILY PRACTICE: THREE PERSPECTIVES

Select an object from your nature museum and draw it from the following three perspectives: lying down, standing up, and flying. Lying down gives you a close-up view that allows the object to fill your drawing space. Drawing while standing of course helps you see how the object appears from above, but you'll want to include anything else in your view from that perspective. How do you draw while flying? Well, picture yourself high above the object and again, draw all that you see. How high is *high* is up to you.

> "To see the world in a grain of sand
> and heaven in a wild flower,
> Hold infinity in the palm of your hand
> and eternity in an hour."
>
> - William Blake

DAY 13 - SIT SPOT JOURNAL

DATE: TIME:

SUNRISE: SUNSET:

MOON PHASE:

WEATHER:

My Intention / Motivation:

What I noticed in nature:

What I noticed within myself:

What this is telling me / teaching me:

Where I see this reflected in my life:

Questions and things to pay attention to:

SIT SPOT JOURNAL

REFLECTION PAGES

CORE ROUTINES OF NATURE AWARENESS

DAILY PRACTICE: KNOW YOUR NEIGHBORS

Today you will visit with your field guides–the elders of the village, the wisdom keepers–in order to fill in the information below. I remind you to try to spend no more than 15 minutes reading and researching and no more than 15 minutes journaling the information.

Select a mammal species local to your area for this exercise.

COMMON NAME   SCIENTIFIC NAME

Draw and label identifying characteristics (field marks), tracks, or anything that interests you about the mammal you have chosen to journal:

Fill in the spaces below from your memory only, if you can.

Physical Description:

Habitat:

Behavior:

Diet:

Range:

Relationship to Native People:

Other Curious Facts:

DAY 14 - SIT SPOT JOURNAL

DATE: TIME:

SUNRISE: SUNSET:

MOON PHASE:

WEATHER:

My Intention / Motivation:

What I noticed in nature:

What I noticed within myself:

What this is telling me / teaching me:

Where I see this reflected in my life:

Questions and things to pay attention to:

SIT SPOT JOURNAL

SIT SPOT AND THE ART OF INNER TRACKING

REFLECTION PAGES

CORE ROUTINES OF NATURE AWARENESS

DAILY PRACTICE - GET CREATIVE!

Use the space provided in any way that will help you deepen your relationship to your Sit Spot, nature, and yourself. Jot down poems, songs, maps, words of thanksgiving, notes, questions, a Sit Spot story–whatever you feel inspired to do!

"Humankind has not woven the web of life.
We are but one thread within it.
Whatever we do to the web, we do to ourselves.
All things are bound together. All things connect."

- Chief Seattle, 1854

DAY 15 - SIT SPOT JOURNAL

DATE: TIME:

SUNRISE: SUNSET:

MOON PHASE:

WEATHER:

My Intention / Motivation:

What I noticed in nature:

What I noticed within myself:

What this is telling me / teaching me:

Where I see this reflected in my life:

Questions and things to pay attention to:

SIT SPOT JOURNAL

REFLECTION PAGES

CORE ROUTINES OF NATURE AWARENESS

DAILY PRACTICE: SHADOWTUDE GRATITUDE

Sometimes it's the very things we resist and fear that have the most to offer us if we can learn to look at them in a different light. Create a list of some of the things in nature that you dislike or even fear: poison ivy, cold rainy days, mosquitos—anything you generally don't appreciate. Once you have your list, read through it and notice how you feel at the thought of each thing. Next, write out as many "positive" aspects of each "shadow" that you can authentically be thankful for. Notice how you feel as you do this.

Example:

Pricker bushes: they provide shelter for small creatures, many bare edible berries for birds and mammals, they create hard-to-explore places that are often interesting to investigare, they teach me to slow down and pay attention, they serve as a favorite nesting site for many of my favorite birds.

"I ask all blessings,
I ask them with reverence,
of my mother the earth,
of the sky, moon and sun my father.
I am old age; the essence of life;
I am the source of all happiness.
All is peaceful, all in beauty,
all in harmony, all in joy."

- Navajo prayer

DAY 16 - SIT SPOT JOURNAL

DATE: TIME:

SUNRISE: SUNSET:

MOON PHASE:

WEATHER:

My Intention / Motivation:

What I noticed in nature:

What I noticed within myself:

What this is telling me / teaching me:

Where I see this reflected in my life:

Questions and things to pay attention to:

SIT SPOT JOURNAL

REFLECTION PAGES

CORE ROUTINES OF NATURE AWARENESS

DAILY PRACTICE: THE SENSE MEDITATION

Just as we can fine-tune our ability to see and hear, so too can we heighten our senses of smell and touch. Perhaps you have naturally begun to do this at your Sit Spot. Here's another opportunity to develop your senses of smell and touch this week; you'll combine them with your ability to see and hear in the big sensory awareness enchilada known as the Sense Meditation.

FIRST: The next time you've settled in at your Sit Spot, close your eyes and take a few deep and relaxing breaths. Open your eyes and go into your soft, wide-angle vision (Owl Eyes), taking in as much as you can.

SECOND: While remaining in your wide-angle vision, begin to allow all the different sounds around you to fill your awareness. "See" the sounds, recognizing their different qualities, textures, densities and intensities, all while maintaining your soft gaze upon the landscape.

THIRD: With both your sight and hearing fully in the "on" position, open yourself up to your sense of touch. Notice how the different parts of your body are experiencing the environment. Feel the wind on your face, the sun's warmth, the way your feet feel in your shoes, and so on.

FOURTH: Next, while keeping your other senses working attentively, add to your awareness the variety of smells that surround you: the trees, the earth, the air, your clothes, and so on. Being so closely linked to your fifth sense, don't be surprised if you actually begin to "taste" the different smells that you're picking up on.

By turning "on" your heightened state of sensory awareness, you have effectively turned off the chattering, busy mind that has likely distracted you from seeing the beauty that is all around you.

Welcome to your quiet mind.

Challenge: The real challenge is to maintain quiet mind for as long as you can. If you find your inner dialog interrupting you with impulsive complaints about the weather, or better things you could be doing with your time, work on turning it off by beginning the sense meditation over again. Your "thinking mind" cannot coexist when you are in full sensory awareness. This doesn't mean that you don't think, but rather, it brings your thinking into the present moment–a place where yesterday and tomorrow don't belong. Confusing? It's not, really; see for yourself. Oh, and while you're at it, consider the following.

It has been said, "The mind is a wonderful servant but a terrible master." How might this statement relate to the difference between a "thinking mind" and a "quiet mind?"

Where in your life is the thinking mind not serving you and what state of being might serve as an effective replacement? How and why?

DAY 17 - SIT SPOT JOURNAL

DATE: TIME:

SUNRISE: SUNSET:

MOON PHASE:

WEATHER:

My Intention / Motivation:

What I noticed in nature:

What I noticed within myself:

What this is telling me / teaching me:

Where I see this reflected in my life:

Questions and things to pay attention to:

SIT SPOT JOURNAL

REFLECTION PAGES

CORE ROUTINES OF NATURE AWARENESS

DAILY PRACTICE: MAPPING BIRDS AND MAMMALS

On this week's map, after laying out the basic landmarks of your Sit Spot, identify places where you know there is evidence of bird and mammal activity. "How am I going to do this one?" you ask. After all, it's not as if the animals are rooted to the ground. Ah, but their tracks and sign are. Notice the robin's nest in the shrub by the house, the raccoon tracks along the stream bank, that funny little pile of droppings under the spruce tree, even the weird teeth marks that run along the base of the old grandfather tulip tree that you sit up against. It's all fair game. Note what you can for now and feel free to add more as you see more. Remember, it's your map, so you get to make the rules.

DAY 18 - SIT SPOT JOURNAL

DATE: TIME:

SUNRISE: SUNSET:

MOON PHASE:

WEATHER:

My Intention / Motivation:

What I noticed in nature:

What I noticed within myself:

What this is telling me / teaching me:

Where I see this reflected in my life:

Questions and things to pay attention to:

SIT SPOT JOURNAL

REFLECTION PAGES

CORE ROUTINES OF NATURE AWARENESS

DAILY PRACTICE: AWARENESS CHALLENGE

You're probably really getting to know your Sit Spot by now, but we all have our blind spots and areas we don't pay attention to. Here are a few questions to ponder to help you know what you know as well as know what you don't know, you know?

What are three species of birds common to your Sit Spot area?

What is the prevailing wind direction at your Sit Spot?

How many paces does it take to get from your Sit Spot to your door?

When was the last time it rained at your Sit Spot?

From the very place you sit, what is the closest mammal track/sign that you've observed and what was it?

Where is the nearest source of water to where you sit (naturally occurring or man-made)?

Where was the last place the moon rose in relation to your Sit Spot?

What direction do you most commonly face while sitting?

What is the most common wild edible plant within 100 feet of your Sit Spot?

Without looking back, how many times did I used the word "'spot" on the previous page?

What else do you know about your Sit Spot?

DAY 19 - SIT SPOT JOURNAL

DATE: TIME:

SUNRISE: SUNSET:

MOON PHASE:

WEATHER:

My Intention / Motivation:

What I noticed in nature:

What I noticed within myself:

What this is telling me / teaching me:

Where I see this reflected in my life:

Questions and things to pay attention to:

SIT SPOT JOURNAL

REFLECTION PAGES

CORE ROUTINES OF NATURE AWARENESS

DAILY PRACTICE: SPIRIT DRAWINGS

Sometimes, as writer Terry Pratchett says, "It's not what a thing is, it's what it be." Select one or more of the natural objects that you have collected for your nature museum, and draw it–only this time, draw its essence, its energy, its spirit!

DAY 20 - SIT SPOT JOURNAL

DATE: TIME:

SUNRISE: SUNSET:

MOON PHASE:

WEATHER:

My Intention / Motivation:

What I noticed in nature:

What I noticed within myself:

What this is telling me / teaching me:

Where I see this reflected in my life:

Questions and things to pay attention to:

SIT SPOT JOURNAL

REFLECTION PAGES

CORE ROUTINES OF NATURE AWARENESS

DAILY PRACTICE: KNOW YOUR NEIGHBORS

It's time to turn once again to your field guides, the elders of the village, the wisdom keepers. Visit with them in order to fill in the information below. Try spending no more than 15 minutes reading and researching and no more than 15 minutes journaling the information.

Select a plant or wildflower species local to your area for this exercise.

COMMON NAME   SCIENTIFIC NAME

Draw and label identifying characteristics (field marks), leaves, and flowers:

Fill in the spaces below from your memory only, if you can.

Physical Description:

Habitat:

Associated plants and animals:

Edible and Medicinal Uses:

Relationship to Native People:

Other Curious Facts:

DAY 21 - SIT SPOT JOURNAL

DATE: TIME:

SUNRISE: SUNSET:

MOON PHASE:

WEATHER:

My Intention / Motivation:

What I noticed in nature:

What I noticed within myself:

What this is telling me / teaching me:

Where I see this reflected in my life:

Questions and things to pay attention to:

SIT SPOT JOURNAL

REFLECTION PAGES

CORE ROUTINES OF NATURE AWARENESS

DAILY PRACTICE: GET CREATIVE!

Use the space provided in any way that will help you deepen your relationship to your Sit Spot, nature, and yourself. Jot down poems, songs, maps, words of thanksgiving, notes, questions, a Sit Spot story—whatever you feel inspired to do!

"And while I stood there I saw more than I can tell
and I understood more than I saw;
for I was seeing in a sacred manner
the shapes of things in the spirit,
and the shape of all shapes as they must live
together like one being."

- Black Elk,
Black Elk Speaks

DAY 22 - SIT SPOT JOURNAL

DATE: TIME:

SUNRISE: SUNSET:

MOON PHASE:

WEATHER:

My Intention / Motivation:

What I noticed in nature:

What I noticed within myself:

What this is telling me / teaching me:

Where I see this reflected in my life:

Questions and things to pay attention to:

SIT SPOT JOURNAL

REFLECTION PAGES

CORE ROUTINES OF NATURE AWARENESS

DAILY PRACTICE: GRATITUDE

In the center of the page, write down your favorite meal or thing to eat. Around that, write down all the things that support the creation of your favorite meal. Extending out from each of these, identify all the things that support their existence. Have fun with this one! Really try to take in the vast, intricate web of ways in which you're supported. If it feels good, send out some words of thanks for those things.

"When we tug at a single thing in nature
we find it attached to the rest of the world."

- John Muir

DAY 23 - SIT SPOT JOURNAL

DATE: TIME:

SUNRISE: SUNSET:

MOON PHASE:

WEATHER:

My Intention / Motivation:

What I noticed in nature:

What I noticed within myself:

What this is telling me / teaching me:

Where I see this reflected in my life:

Questions and things to pay attention to:

SIT SPOT JOURNAL

REFLECTION PAGES

CORE ROUTINES OF NATURE AWARENESS

DAILY PRACTICE: FOX WALKING

Have you been practicing your Sense Meditation? If you have, you might be feeling like something of a sensory Jedi by now, but wait! There's more! Yes, more! How can this be, you ask? Well, as much as being still at your Sit Spot and turning up the sensory volume is cool, turning down the volume knob on the noise and energy that is displaced on the way to your Sit Spot can be equally cool. Picture, if you will, a still, clear pond. Now, imagine throwing a large boulder into the pond. What happens? Exactly–it creates a disturbance that can be seen in the form of concentric rings that radiate out from the place where the boulder hit the water. Guess what? That's exactly what you create with every footstep that you take on the way to your Sit Spot. But don't worry, we can fix that with just a few simple steps: fox steps.

Because of the shoes we wear, most of us have learned to walk heel to toe, rather than toe to heel, as we're anatomically designed to walk. Because of this, not only are ankle, knee, and back problems common in people, but we rarely ever get close to seeing wildlife because they sense our approach. Fox Walking will help change that.

FIRST: With your head up and facing forward, prepare to take a step forward by putting all of your weight on your left leg.

SECOND: Now, lift your right leg s-l-o-w-l-y (really slowly—we're talking 30 seconds to complete one step). Gently place the outside part of your right foot to the ground but keep all of your weight on the left leg.

THIRD: Keeping your right heel still in the air, slowly and gently roll your toes and the front part your foot onto the ground and use them to sense what's below your foot.

FOURTH: Next, slowly roll the rest of your foot to the ground. Once your foot is completely on the ground, only then should you shift your weight to your right leg. Congratulations! You're Fox

Walking! All you have left to do is take a step with the other foot and repeat as needed (which you may find is all of the time).

Challenge: To really get how it works, try Fox Walking barefoot. Once you think you've got the hang of it, start Fox Walking to and from your Sit Spot. If you really want to blow your mind, practice the sense meditation while Fox Walking. Remember, the goal is to cast off as few and as small concentric rings as possible so as not to cause a disturbance in the Force! Use the force, Luke, don't disturb it! Here's some food for thought.

How might Fox Walking have served as an imperative skill for our native ancestors?

In what ways might Fox Walking be a valuable tool in today's world?

Metaphorically speaking, where in your life might Fox Walking gain you access to the things you desire most and how might the opposite form of walking through life have kept you from what you want?

DAY 24 - SIT SPOT JOURNAL

DATE: TIME:

SUNRISE: SUNSET:

MOON PHASE:

WEATHER:

My Intention / Motivation:

What I noticed in nature:

What I noticed within myself:

What this is telling me / teaching me:

Where I see this reflected in my life:

Questions and things to pay attention to:

SIT SPOT JOURNAL

REFLECTION PAGES

CORE ROUTINES OF NATURE AWARENESS

DAILY PRACTICE: MAPPING

It's your Sit Spot and this is your Sit Spot journal, so you choose what you want to map. Everything. Nothing. Perhaps the incredible, interconnected, subnivian super-highway that runs all over the backyard that seems to expose itself only on warm days in January. What the heck is "subnivian," anyway? Maybe it would be fun to let your heart choose for you, by paying attention to what really speaks to you when you go to your Sit Spot. Just sayin', is all.

DAY 25 - SIT SPOT JOURNAL

DATE: TIME:

SUNRISE: SUNSET:

MOON PHASE:

WEATHER:

My Intention / Motivation:

What I noticed in nature:

What I noticed within myself:

What this is telling me / teaching me:

Where I see this reflected in my life:

Questions and things to pay attention to:

SIT SPOT JOURNAL

REFLECTION PAGES

CORE ROUTINES OF NATURE AWARENESS

DAILY PRACTICE: AWARENESS CHALLENGE

People who are truly "native" to their environment have a remarkable knowledge of the land they live upon; after all, their lives depend upon that knowledge. For many of us, however, knowing what's in the contained space of our refrigerator is challenging enough. Or is it? On the page below, create a list of all the things that can be found on the shelves and in the drawers of your refrigerator at this very moment. No peeking. Should you be feeling feisty, use the adjacent page to map out the location of each item. Afterward, go see how you made out. As for the freezer, well... who knows what lurks in there?

DAY 26 - SIT SPOT JOURNAL

DATE: TIME:

SUNRISE: SUNSET:

MOON PHASE:

WEATHER:

My Intention / Motivation:

What I noticed in nature:

What I noticed within myself:

What this is telling me / teaching me:

Where I see this reflected in my life:

Questions and things to pay attention to:

SIT SPOT JOURNAL

REFLECTION PAGES

CORE ROUTINES OF NATURE AWARENESS

DAILY PRACTICE: DRAW WHAT YOU FEEL

Take several objects from your nature museum and put them in a bag or under a sheet so you can touch the objects but can't look at them. Keeping the objects out of sight, select one and spend a minute or two getting to know it through your sense of touch only. When you're satisfied that you know the object, draw it without looking at it. Afterward, look at the object you drew and make notes on what you learned. For fun, you might want to invite a friend to identify the object you drew by allowing him or her to see your drawing, but selecting the correct object using their sense of touch only.

"Midnight. No waves, no wind,
the empty boat is flooded with moonlight."

- Dogen

DAY 27 - SIT SPOT JOURNAL

DATE: TIME:

SUNRISE: SUNSET:

MOON PHASE:

WEATHER:

My Intention / Motivation:

What I noticed in nature:

What I noticed within myself:

What this is telling me / teaching me:

Where I see this reflected in my life:

Questions and things to pay attention to:

SIT SPOT JOURNAL

REFLECTION PAGES

CORE ROUTINES OF NATURE AWARENESS

DAILY PRACTICE: KNOW YOUR NEIGHBORS

It's time to turn once again to your field guides, the elders of the village, the wisdom keepers. Visit with them in order to fill in the information below. Try spending no more than 15 minutes reading and researching and no more than 15 minutes journaling the information.

Select a tree species local to your area for this exercise.

COMMON NAME   SCIENTIFIC NAME

Draw and label identifying characteristics (field marks), leaves, flowers, cones, fruits, or nuts:

Fill in the spaces below from your memory only, if you can.

Physical Description:

Habitat:

Associated plants and animals:

Edible and Medicinal Uses:

Relationship to Native People:

Other Curious Facts:

DAY 28 - SIT SPOT JOURNAL

DATE: TIME:

SUNRISE: SUNSET:

MOON PHASE:

WEATHER:

My Intention / Motivation:

What I noticed in nature:

What I noticed within myself:

What this is telling me / teaching me:

Where I see this reflected in my life:

Questions and things to pay attention to:

SIT SPOT JOURNAL

REFLECTION PAGES

CORE ROUTINES OF NATURE AWARENESS

DAILY PRACTICE: GET CREATIVE!

Use the space provided in any way that will help you deepen your relationship to your Sit Spot, nature, and yourself. Jot down poems, songs, maps, words of thanksgiving, notes, questions, a Sit Spot story—whatever you feel inspired to do!

"In simplicity there is unlimited power."

- Stalking Wolf

DAY 29 - SIT SPOT JOURNAL

DATE: TIME:

SUNRISE: SUNSET:

MOON PHASE:

WEATHER:

My Intention / Motivation:

What I noticed in nature:

What I noticed within myself:

What this is telling me / teaching me:

Where I see this reflected in my life:

Questions and things to pay attention to:

SIT SPOT JOURNAL

REFLECTION PAGES

CORE ROUTINES OF NATURE AWARENESS

DAILY PRACTICE: HONORING AND COMMITMENTS

As you approach the threshold of completing the 30-Day Sit Spot Challenge, it is important to take some time to reflect upon your accomplishments and to honor yourself for your achievements. This is also a good time to consider how you'd like to continue to develop and strengthen the threads of relationship that you've been creating and developing between yourself and your Sit Spot.

Use the space provided to honor yourself for all that you've achieved. What did it feel like to venture into uncharted territory and learn new things? What did it feel like to allow yourself to grow and heal from whatever you've learned? What risks did you take? How can you thank yourself for the inner and outer work you've done? Notice how it feels to do this. Is it difficult for you to say nice things about yourself? Does it feel awkward? Just pay attention to what comes up and make a note of it. Also, write out any commitments to yourself that you would like to make regarding future Sit Spots and developing a deeper connection to nature, yourself, and others. When you write your commitments out, make sure they're observable and measurable with clear parameters. For example: *I will go to my Sit Spot at least twice a week, for a minimum of one half-hour each time, for the next year.* You may even wish to put this list of commitments up in a place where you'll see it, as a friendly reminder.

DAY 30 - SIT SPOT JOURNAL

DATE: TIME:

SUNRISE: SUNSET:

MOON PHASE:

WEATHER:

My Intention / Motivation:

What I noticed in nature:

What I noticed within myself:

What this is telling me / teaching me:

Where I see this reflected in my life:

Questions and things to pay attention to:

SIT SPOT JOURNAL

REFLECTION PAGES

CORE ROUTINES OF NATURE AWARENESS

DAILY PRACTICE: GRATITUDE

You've made it to the end of your 30-Day Sit Spot Challenge. Congratulations! This would be the perfect opportunity to thank the seen and unseen forces and beings that supported you on your journey. Take a moment to think of all that you've learned from your Sit Spot. Consider the new connections that you've made with the earth and the old connections that you've strengthened. Consider, too, the connections that you were able to release, the ones that were no longer serving you. How did going to your Sit Spot support you in this and for what do you find yourself feeling gratitude?

"A hand moves, and the fire's whirling
takes different shapes:
All things change when we do.
The first word "Ah,"
blossoms into all others.
Each of them is true."

- Kukai

ABOUT THE AUTHOR

R. Michael Trotta, MPS is an artist, storyteller, learning specialist, master coach, survival skills expert, student of native traditions and the Hero's Journey, proud dyslexic, facilitator of rites of passage programs, community builder and coffee lover who lives to create culture that connects people to their "Original Medicine." Michael co-founded the Sagefire Institute with his wife Lynn in 2005 and currently enjoys enriching a wide variety of coaching and educational training programs by lending his own special blend of myth and mischief to the mix. Michael was raised by coyotes and is now happily raising one of his own.

For more information on his work and programs visit:

www.SagefireInstitute.com

Made in the USA
Lexington, KY
22 August 2017